Caring

by Lucia Raatma

CHERRY LAKE PUBLISHING * ANN ARBOR, MICHIGAN

Published in the United States of America by Cherry Lake Publishing
Ann Arbor, Michigan
www.cherrylakepublishing.com

Content Adviser: David Wangaard, Executive Director, SEE: The School for Ethical Education, Milford, Connecticut

Reading Adviser: Marla Conn, ReadAbility, Inc.

Photo Credits: Cover and page 12, ©Monkey Business Images/Shutterstock, Inc.; page 4, ©Gladskikh Tatiana/Shutterstock, Inc.; page 6, ©Andresr/Dreamstime.com; page 8, ©Kzenon/Shutterstock, Inc.; page 10, ©Yuri Arcurs/Shutterstock, Inc.; page 14, ©Intst/Dreamstime.com; page 16, ©Design Pics Inc./Alamy; page 18, ©Diego Cervo/Shutterstock, Inc.; page 20, ©Mircea Netval/Shutterstock, Inc.

LIBRARY OF CONGRESS CATALOGING-IN-PUBLICATION DATA
Raatma, Lucia.
  Caring/by Lucia Raatma.
    pages cm.—(Character education) (21st century junior library)
  Includes bibliographical references and index.
  ISBN 978-1-62431-153-6 (lib. bdg.)—ISBN 978-1-62431-219-9 (e-book)—
ISBN 978-1-62431-285-4 (pbk.)
  1. Caring—Juvenile literature. I. Title.
  BJ1475.R33 2013
  177'.7—dc23   2013004804

*Cherry Lake Publishing would like to acknowledge the work of
The Partnership for 21st Century Skills.
Please visit www.p21.org for more information.*

Printed in the United States of America
Corporate Graphics Inc.
July 2013
CLFA13

CONTENTS

Your friends and family show they care by cheering you up when you are sad.

What Is Caring?

Steven sighed and rested his head in his hands as he sat down after getting home from school. "What's the matter?" asked his dad.

"I had a bad day today," said Steven.

"Do you want to talk about it while we shoot some hoops?" Steven's dad asked with a smile.

"Yeah!" he answered. "Thanks, Dad."

It is easy to make friends when you are a caring person.

When you are caring, you see what other people need. You take action to help them. You think about how your actions will help or hurt someone. A caring person chooses not to be selfish, mean, or hurtful.

Think!

Remember a time when someone was mean to you. How did their actions make you feel? Now remember a time when someone was kind to you. What did they do for you? How did you feel then?

Your parents do a lot for you. Show you care by helping out around the house.

Being a Caring Person

There are many ways to show that you care at home. Alex likes to spend time playing with his brothers and sisters. He helps them with any problems they are having.

A person can also be caring to his or her parents. Susan always listens to them when they talk to her. She also helps them out with chores.

Always say "thank you" when someone
gives you a gift.

A caring person chooses not to hurt other people's feelings. John's grandma bought him a new shirt that he didn't like. But he didn't want to hurt her feelings. He was caring by thanking her and wearing the shirt anyway.

Sarah's older sister got a silly haircut. Sarah chose not to make fun of it. Instead, she cheers her sister up and says her hair will grow back quickly.

Be friendly to your classmates at school.

There are many ways to be caring at school. Emma made friends with a new student who was sitting alone. Will brought homework assignments to a friend who was home sick from school. Caring people don't **bully** or tease others. Instead, they help friends stand up to bullies.

Create!

Talk with your family about caring. Make a list of kind things you can do. Maybe you can make a get-well card for a sick friend. Or tell your mom she looks nice when she dresses up to go out. Write down how people react to your caring actions.

Helping your neighbors shovel snow is a great way to show you care.

People can be caring in their neighborhood. Ethan likes to know the people who live around him. He made friends with other kids in the neighborhood. He helps neighbors shovel snow or care for their yards.

Sometimes Abby's neighbors go on trips. She offers to feed or walk their pets when they are away.

Your old clothing could be very useful to people in need.

Caring for Your World

There are probably many people in your community who are in need. You can **volunteer** to help. You could donate food to a **food pantry**. Groups that help people also may need help. You could volunteer at the animal **shelter**.

Recycling helps keep our planet healthy.

A person can also choose to care for the **planet**. Sophie does this by **recycling** paper, bottles, cans, and other materials.

Why not plant flowers and bushes in the yard? They provide food and shelter for insects and other animals. People will enjoy their beauty.

Look!

If you pay attention, you will see people helping others. Keep your eyes open. You're sure to find many ways to lend a hand.

If you care for other people, they will care for you.

When you are caring, you make other people feel special. They know that they are important to you. As you act in caring ways, you spread good feelings. Choose to do your part to make the world a more caring place.

Make a Guess!

What would happen if you were kind to everyone you saw? How do you think others would react? Try it! Smile at the people you pass in the hallway. Offer to help someone carry a heavy package. Share your candy or gum with your friends. Did people react the way you thought they would?

GLOSSARY

bully (BULL-ee) to scare or pick on people who are weaker than you

food pantry (FOOD PAN-tree) an organization that collects donations of food and then gives the food to people who are hungry and can't afford to buy it

planet (PLAN-it) one of the eight large bodies that circle the sun; Earth is a planet

recycling (ree-SYE-kuhl-ing) processing old items so they can be used to make new products

shelter (SHEL-tur) a place where people or animals can stay to be safe and protected from danger

volunteer (vol-uhn-TIHR) offer to do a job for no pay

FIND OUT MORE

BOOKS

Cuyler, Margery. *Kindess Is Cooler, Mrs. Ruler*. New York: Simon and Schuster Books for Young Readers, 2007.

Snow, Todd, and Peggy Snow. *Kindness to Share from A to Z*. Oak Park Heights, MN: Maren Green Publishing, Inc., 2008.

WEB SITE

Community Service: A Family's Guide
http://kidshealth.org/parent /positive/family/volunteer.html#
Find out how you and your family can help out in your community.

INDEX

ABOUT THE AUTHOR

Lucia Raatma has written dozens of books for young readers. They are about famous people, historical events, ways to stay safe, and other topics. She lives in Florida's Tampa Bay area with her husband and their two children.